THE FARCE OF PROGRESS

By Eli Andrade

Copyright © 2026 by Eli Andrade
All rights reserved.

No part of this book may be reproduced in any form or by any electronic or mechanical means, including information storage and retrieval systems, without permission in writing from the author, except by a reviewer who may quote brief passages in a review.

This is a work of fiction/non-fiction. Names, characters, places, and incidents either are the products of the author's imagination or are used fictitiously. Any resemblance to actual persons, living or dead, businesses, companies, events, or locales is entirely coincidental.

ISBN: 979-82-49263-83-6
Edition: First Edition
Published by: Eli Andrade
Year: 2026

CONTENTS

PART 1 — THE PANICKED ANTHILL 4
   1. The Illusion of Progress 5
   2. The Cycle of Exhaustion 12
   3. The Price of Being Alive 18

PART 2 — THE PRISON OF GLASS AND 25
   4. The Golden Cage of Convenience 26
   5. The Filter of Dissatisfaction 32
   6. The Cry of the Sou 39

PART 3 — THE MARKET OF INSECURITY 43
   7. Connected and Lonely 44
   8. The Bandage Industry 49
   9. The Myth of Infinite Growth 53

PART 4 — LEAVING THE GAME 56
   10. Recognizing the Farce 57
   11. Living by Your Own Rules 62
   12. The Only Real Currency: Time 66

PART 1
The Panicked Anthill

CHAPTER 1

The Illusion of Progress

If you could float in the black vacuum of space, far enough away to ignore political borders but close enough to observe the pulse of lights, what you would see would not be a civilization advancing toward a glorious destiny. You would see a panicked anthill. You would see a frenetic mass of eight billion organisms running in concentric circles, driven by an invisible yet relentless force. From a distance, the Earth looks serene; up close, it vibrates with the static of billions of minds that have forgotten how to breathe without feeling guilt.

We call this progress. We love that word. It has a metallic, clean, almost sacred sound. Progress is the modern religion, and Gross Domestic Product is its god. But if we stop to analyze the mechanics of this advancement, we realize that human progress, in its current form, is the greatest piece of fiction ever written by our species. It is a collective optical illusion, where we mistake speed for direction and movement for purpose.

We are running. Running hard. But where to? And more importantly, why are we running so fast that we can no longer even look to the side?

The Conversion of Life into Paper

The great magic trick of the 21st century was convincing us that our existence is a commodity that needs to be mined, refined, and sold. We have transformed time—the only thing we truly possess from the moment of birth until our last breath—into a crude currency.

Think about your average day. You wake up to the sound of an alarm. That sound is not an invitation to life; it is a command from a system that demands your presence. It is the first sign that your time does not belong to you. You get up, often still exhausted, and begin the ritual of preparing yourself to be "productive." We drink coffee not for the flavor, but to start the engines of a biological machine that is screaming for two more hours of sleep.

Then, we enter metal or plastic cans—buses, trains, cars—and compress ourselves with other human beings who feel the exact same contempt for the present moment. We cross the city to reach a cubicle, a store, a factory, or a computer screen, where we will spend the best daylight hours of our day. And why do we do this?

To convert those hours into numbers in a bank account.

We spend forty, fifty, sixty hours a week transforming our vital energy into paper money. And then, in an act of cruel irony, we use that paper money to buy the right to survive and to acquire objects that help us forget how much we hate the process of earning the money. We buy bigger televisions to anesthetize ourselves at night. We buy clothes that tell others we are successful when, in truth, we are just exhausted. We buy gadgets that promise to save the time we've already wasted.

We have become the only animals on planet Earth that **pay to live here**. The bird does not pay for the branch where it perches. The lion does not pay rent for the savannah. The fish does not need a monthly subscription to swim in the ocean. But the human being, the "crown of creation," is born in debt. From the first cry, the meter is running. You have to pay for air (if you want it filtered), for water, for land, and for a roof. If you don't have the paper money, the system discards you.

Progress, then, is not about the liberation of man. It is about the refinement of his slavery. In the past, chains were made of iron and were visible. Today, they are made of bills, sales targets, and the desperate need to maintain a standard of living that we didn't even choose.

The Cycle of Performative Exhaustion

We live in the era of performance. It is no longer enough to be a good professional, a good parent, or a good citizen. You need to **look** like all of that in high definition. Progress gave us communication tools that were supposed to bring us closer, but ended up creating a permanent stage where no one can afford to step out of character.

Observe people in a café or on public transport. Almost everyone is hunched over small luminous rectangles. We are physically present, but our minds are elsewhere, mining dopamine on social networks. We are comparing our "backstage"—our mess, our sadness, our fatigue—with the edited "highlight reels" of strangers.

This constant comparison feeds the engine of capitalist progress. The system needs you to feel inadequate. It needs you to feel that your house is too small, your body is imperfect, your vacation was mediocre, and that you are falling behind. Happy, fulfilled people are terrible for the economy. People who feel complete do not feel the compulsive need to buy a new car to fill an existential void.

Therefore, the illusion of progress is maintained by a manufactured anxiety. The anxiety that, if we stop running, the world will collapse upon us. We created a vocabulary for this madness: "hustle culture," "burnout," "FOMO" (the fear of missing out). At their core, these are just modern names for the panic of a species that has lost touch with the rhythm of nature and chained itself to the rhythm of the algorithm.

We have turned life into a career. And a career, by definition, is a race. But nobody tells us where the finish line is. When you get the raise, you need another. When you buy the house, you need the renovation. Progress is a line on the horizon: you walk toward it, and it recedes in the same proportion. It is the torment of Tantalus redesigned for the digital age.

The Golden Cage of Convenience

Often, when we question this lifestyle, someone points to the past and says: "But look how we've evolved! We have antibiotics, the internet, and air conditioning. Would you rather live in the Middle Ages and die of the bubonic plague at thirty?"

This is the favorite logical trap of the defenders of the *status quo*. Of course, medical and technological advances are valuable. However, the error lies in believing that to have penicillin, we must accept the destruction of our mental health and the commercialization of every second of our existence. Technological progress should not be a Faustian bargain, where we surrender our soul and our peace in exchange for fast Wi-Fi and home food delivery.

We have created a golden cage made of convenience. Everything is easy, everything is clickable, everything is delivered to your door. But this convenience has a hidden price: the atrophy of our capacity to be. We are biological animals. We evolved over millions of years to be in motion, in contact with the earth, embedded in small and meaningful communities, and surrounded by the cycles of the sun and the seasons.

Instead, we spend our days in climate-controlled environments with fluorescent lights, sitting in ergonomic chairs that try to compensate for the fact that our bodies were not made to be bent at ninety degrees for eight hours straight. We eat processed foods designed in labs to addict our palates, while taking pills to lower the blood pressure and control the cholesterol that the lifestyle itself caused.

We are living in a human zoo that we built ourselves. And, like caged animals, we begin to show erratic behaviors. We gnaw at the bars. We get depressed. We become aggressive toward one other. We increase the doses of our antidepressants and anxiolytics just to be able to bear the weight of a "normal life."

If you need medication to endure your routine, perhaps the problem isn't your brain chemistry. Perhaps your brain chemistry is the only sane thing about you, desperately signaling that the environment you live in is toxic. Anxiety is not a system error; it is a fire alarm.

The Invisible Cost of "More"

The illusion of progress is based on the premise of infinite growth. Companies need to grow every year. The economy needs to expand. You need to have more this year than you had last year.

But we live on a finite planet. There is a limit to how much we can extract, how much we can consume, and how much waste we can generate. And there is, above all, a limit to the human psyche.

We sacrifice our community at the altar of profit. In the past, people depended on each other. Today, we depend on services. If you need something, you don't ask your neighbor; you pay a corporation. This has made us "independent," but also terribly lonely. We have five thousand friends on Facebook, but we have no one to help us carry a sofa or to listen to our pains without charging by the hour.

We trade our purpose for productivity. The goal of life is no longer to flourish as an individual, but to be an efficient part in the machine. If you spend an entire afternoon looking at the clouds or reading poetry without "producing" anything, you feel a weight in your chest. The system has trained us to feel that rest is a sin and that idleness is a crime against humanity.

But the truth is that the best things in life do not produce GDP. A long hug does not generate profit. Watching the sunset does not increase any company's stock. Playing with your child on the grass is an economic disaster because you are not consuming anything. The system hates what is free and what is simple, because it cannot tax simplicity.

The Farce of Success

We look at the people at the top of the pyramid and call them "winners." We admire the CEO who sleeps four hours a night, who lives on planes, and who has billions of dollars. But if you look closely, you will often see a man or a woman who doesn't know their own children, whose body is on the verge of collapse, and whose mind is a whirlwind of stress and paranoia.

If success requires you to sacrifice your health, your peace of mind, and your time with those you love, then it is not success. It is a defeat disguised as a trophy.

The illusion of progress makes us believe that happiness is always in the next step. In the next promotion. In the next iPhone. In the next house. We are always "preparing" to live, but we never actually live. Life is always something that is going to happen after we finish this project, after we pay this debt, after the kids grow up.

Meanwhile, time—the real gold—slips through our fingers.

Eight billion panicked ants. Running to turn sun into shadow, forest into concrete, and silence into noise. We call this civilization. We call this evolution. But if you take a step back and look at your own hands, at your own chest, you will feel the truth.

You are not a data processor. You are not a consumer. You are not a "human resource."

You are a biological miracle breathing on a planet floating in nothingness. You have a finite number of heartbeats remaining. And every second you spend being a cog in a machine that doesn't love you, doesn't know you, and would replace you in 24 hours if you died, is a betrayal of your own existence.

The farce of progress is making us believe we have no choice. It is convincing us that this is the only possible path. But the anthill only stays in a panic as long as each ant believes the race is necessary.

What would happen if you stopped? What would happen if you decided that "enough" is truly enough?

The world would not end. The system would tremble, yes, because it depends on your dissatisfaction to survive. But for the first time, you might hear the sound of your own heart. And you would realize that true progress is not going further, faster, or higher. True progress is being able to return to yourself.

We are all pretending. We pretend this is normal. We pretend that infinite growth on a finite planet is possible. We pretend we are happy while the world burns around us, physically and metaphorically. But the illusion only works if you keep your eyes closed.

This book is not about how to win the game. It is about realizing the game is a farce and having the courage to stand up from the table. Because, in the end, the only thing that truly belongs to us is the time between our first and our last breath. And spending that time being a part in a machine that doesn't love you is the greatest tragedy of all.

Welcome to the first step out of the anthill. It may be scary, but for the first time, the ground beneath your feet will be real. And time—that time you used to sell for so little—will finally begin to be yours again.

CHAPTER 2

The Cycle of Exhaustion

Sound is not merely a noise; it is a violation. At six-thirty in the morning, or perhaps seven, your smartphone blares that pre-programmed ringtone which, over the months, has ceased to be a melody and become the trigger for a Pavlovian response of dread. Even before your eyes focus, before your consciousness registers who you are or where you are, your body already knows. Your heart rate quickens slightly. Your jaw tightens. The weight of the world, which had been gently set aside during a few hours of restless sleep, crashes down upon your chest once again.

You stretch out your arm. The movement is mechanical, almost a ritualistic prayer of denial. The "Snooze" button is the greatest monument to our futile hope. Five minutes. Ten minutes. As if this tiny hiatus between consciousness and duty could somehow reverse the inevitable fact that the day has begun, and you are already late for a race you never asked to run.

Welcome to the cycle. Welcome to the gear.

What happens in the first sixty minutes of your day defines the tragedy of our modernity. You don't wake up because your body is rested; you wake up because the system needs you. You rise not for a purpose that makes your blood vibrate, but out of a silent, omnipresent fear: the fear of falling behind, the fear of failing to pay the price of your own existence, the fear of being the only ant that stopped carrying the leaf while the rest of the anthill continues its march.

The first thing you do, almost instinctively, is check the screen. The blue light stabs at your still-sleepy retinas. Notifications, emails, news of tragedies miles away, photos of people you barely know faking lives they don't have. In less than five minutes, your mind has been hijacked. You no longer inhabit your own body; you inhabit the demands of others. Exhaustion begins here, before your feet even touch the cold floor.

Then comes the commute. It might be a car trapped in a traffic jam that looks like an artery clogged with metal and smoke, or a subway car where the air is heavy with the breath and weariness of hundreds of other human beings who, like you, are staring into the void. Observe the faces around you tomorrow morning. It is a gallery of ghosts. There is no joy in those eyes, no curiosity. There is only the acceptance of a sentence.

We are all in transit to places we do not want to be. We spend precious hours of our lives—the only truly finite resource we possess—in "non-places." Corridors, highways, stations. All this to reach the altar of productivity. And what do we call productivity? Most of the time, it is merely the act of moving data from one side to the other, of responding to messages that generate more messages, of attending meetings that serve only to schedule the next meeting.

We have transformed survival into an exhaustive performance.

Think about it: we are the only species on the planet that pays to live here. A bird does not pay rent for its tree. A wolf does not need a credit card to hunt. But we, the apex of evolution, the masters of technology, are born owing. We owe for the land we step on, for the water we drink, for the roof that protects us from the rain. And to pay this lifelong debt, we sell our time. But the system is greedy. It doesn't just want your hours; it wants your vital energy, your creativity, and your peace of mind.

We arrive at work and put on our mask. We call this "professionalism." It is the theater of "I'm fine, I'm focused, I'm engaged." But inside, the question echoes: Is this all? We spend eight, ten, twelve hours focused on goals that mean nothing to our souls, to enrich structures that would replace us in five minutes if our hearts stopped beating. And we call this a "career." We put this title in gold letters on LinkedIn and wear it like armor to hide the emptiness growing in our chests.

The cycle of exhaustion is fueled by a fundamental lie: that if we work hard enough today, we can finally rest tomorrow. But tomorrow is a mirage that recedes as we advance.

When the workday finally ends, you don't go home. You go back to what is left of you. The commute back is a painful decompression. You walk through the door and you are empty. There is no energy to play with your children, to read that book that has been on your nightstand for months, or to have a deep conversation with your partner. What do you do? You surrender to the anesthesia.

Modern entertainment consumption is not a leisure choice; it is a survival mechanism. You turn on the television or scroll through social media feeds because these are the only activities that demand nothing from you. It is the "rest of the exhausted," a form of waking coma where you ingest images and sounds to silence the internal screams of dissatisfaction. Capitalism knows this. It creates the weariness and then sells the remedy for that weariness in the form of a streaming subscription, processed food delivery, or online retail therapy to fill the hole that the work itself dug.

"I just need to make it to the weekend," we tell ourselves on Tuesday.

The weekend has become the ultimate consolation prize. Two days of parole to compensate for five days of incarceration. But even the weekend has been colonized by exhaustion. Saturday is the day to handle the chores that your "career" didn't allow for: cleaning the house, going to the supermarket, paying the month's bills. And Sunday? Sunday is haunted by the shadow of Monday. By six o'clock on Sunday evening, the cycle restarts in the mind. Anticipatory anxiety sets in. The opening theme of a Sunday night TV show sounds like the funeral march of your temporary freedom.

Why do we do this? Why do we accept that life be reduced to this sequence of alarms and fatigue?

The answer is as simple as it is terrifying: because we were convinced there is no alternative. We were taught that this is the price of progress. That exhaustion is a badge of honor. If you are exhausted, it means you are important, you are necessary, you are "winning." But look around you. If everyone is winning, why does everyone seem to be losing their sanity?

Depression and anxiety are not isolated biological flaws in an unlucky population; they are logical responses to a pathological environment. If you put a fish in a tank with toxic water, it will get sick. You don't try to "cure" the fish by teaching it to meditate or prescribing it antidepressants so it can better endure the dirty water; you change the water. But our system prefers to sell us bandages. It prefers to call your exhaustion "burnout"—as if you were a lightbulb that simply burned out from over-use—rather than admit that the electrical grid itself is short-circuiting.

The Cycle of Exhaustion works because it keeps us too busy to question our direction. If you are running all the time just to avoid falling off the treadmill, you don't have time to ask who turned on the machine and where it is going. Exhaustion is a tool of control. Exhausted people do not revolt. Exhausted people do not create communities. Exhausted people do not question the status quo. They just buy what is easy, eat what is fast, and sleep whenever possible.

We are sacrificing our biology on the altar of an economy that does not love us. We evolved over millions of years to live in circadian rhythms, to see sunlight, to walk on the earth, to socialize in tribes, to create with our hands. And, in just a few centuries, we threw it all away in exchange for office cubicles and Excel spreadsheets. We traded the outdoors for air conditioning. We traded purpose for productivity.

And what did we gain? More "stuff." We gained the right to own objects we don't have time to use, in houses where we only spend the hours we are unconscious. We work jobs we hate to buy things we don't need to impress people we don't like. That phrase is a cliché for a reason: because it describes the exact architecture of our prison.

The truth is that the progress we were promised is a farce if it requires you to stop being a human and start being a resource. "Human Resources." Have you ever stopped to think about the cruelty of that term? You are not a person; you are a resource, like oil, coal, or timber. Something to be extracted, used, and when it is depleted, discarded.

The exhaustion you feel is not a sign of weakness. It is the healthiest sign your body can give. It is your soul knocking on the door, screaming that this contract is abusive. It is the visceral realization that life should be something more than a marathon of obligations interrupted by periods of induced unconsciousness.

The Cycle of Exhaustion only breaks when you stop running. And to stop running is the most subversive act you can commit in this world. It doesn't necessarily mean quitting your job tomorrow or moving into a cave—though sometimes the idea seems tempting. It means decolonizing your mind. It means understanding that your value is not measured by your productivity. It means reclaiming your time, even if only in small cracks of silence and refusal.

We call this cycle "living." We call it a "career." We call it "normality." But if we look closely, without the lenses of marketing and social pressure, we will see what it really is: a tragic waste of a miraculous existence. You are the result of billions of years of cosmic evolution, of stars that exploded and ancestors who survived ice ages and plagues. You are not here to merely be a battery for the system.

The first step out of the panicked anthill is admitting that you are tired. Not the tiredness a night of sleep can fix, but the tiredness of someone who has realized they are running in circles.

Tomorrow, when the alarm rings, before you hit "Snooze," before you look at your phone, just feel that tiredness. Don't try to escape it. Let it tell you the truth. The cycle only has power over you as long as you believe it is mandatory. But the cage door is open. It always has been. The problem is that we are too exhausted to notice. And that is exactly how the system likes us.

CHAPTER 3

The Price of Being Alive

Imagine, for a moment, a humpback whale calf breaking the icy surface of the ocean in her first breach. She doesn't need a license to swim. She owes the ocean nothing for the krill she consumes. No bank sends her a bill for the oxygen she exchanges in the Southern Seas. Now, look at a wolf crossing the Siberian tundras, or a simple sparrow landing on your windowsill. They inhabit this planet under a simple but radical premise: the Earth is their home, and the right to exist is intrinsic to their birth.

Now, look at yourself—the apex of evolution, the master of technology, the holder of Promethean fire. Look at the Modern Worker in the mirror. Unlike every other of the millions of species that have ever walked, crawled, or flown over this blue rock, you are the only living being that has to **pay to be here**.

Think about the magnitude of this absurdity. We took a planet that was given to us all for free and we subdivided it. We put fences around mountains, pipes in the rivers, and barcodes on the sunlight. We transformed the fundamental act of existing into a full-time financial performance. At the exact instant you let out your first cry in the delivery room, the System's clock began to tick. Before you even learned to say "mother," you were already a debtor. There was a fee for the hospital, a fee for the registration, a cost for the clothes covering your skin, and an invisible debt accumulated by the mere fact that you occupy a three-dimensional space on the Earth's surface.

Welcome to the Panicked Anthill. The admission is expensive, and the stay is charged by the minute.

The System is a sophisticated plantation owner. It no longer uses iron chains; it uses something far more efficient: the necessity of survival converted into currency. We are not just human beings; in the eyes of the machine, we are "Human Resources." And a resource is something to be extracted, processed, and eventually discarded when its usefulness ends.

The System's great trick was convincing you that this is the natural order of things. We look at our electricity bills, our rents, our mortgages, and our taxes as if they were laws of physics—as immutable as gravity. But they aren't. They are artificial constructs designed to keep the battery charged and the machine running. The Modern Worker spends the best years of their life—the years when their body is strong, their mind is sharp, and their spirit is vibrant—in a state of voluntary servitude. We sell our mornings, our afternoons, and often our nights, just to earn the right not to be evicted from our own existence.

It is a perverse form of existential extortion. If you stop producing, the System strips away the layers of protection it created itself. It takes away the roof over your head, the food from your table, and the dignity of your name. Thus, we live in a state of subliminal terror. The anxiety you feel on Sunday night is not an isolated chemical "disorder"; it is the alarm of an animal that knows if it doesn't perform tomorrow, its survival will be at risk.

We have turned life into a subscription service. You subscribe to the right to live, the right to move, the right to communicate, and even the right to have fun. The problem with subscriptions is that they never end. They require a constant feeding of capital. And where do you get that capital? By selling the only thing that truly belongs to you: your time.

Time is the only true currency of the universe. When you buy a luxury car, you don't pay with Reais or Dollars; you pay with the months or years of life you had to sacrifice to obtain that value. You are trading pieces of your biology—heartbeats that will never return—for metal and plastic. And the System loves this trade. It needs you to value the object more than the hours spent to get it, because if you realized the true value of your time, you would become dangerously expensive.

Consider the routine of the Modern Worker. He wakes up before the sun, often ignoring the circadian rhythms that took eons to perfect. He consumes caffeine to force a state of alertness his body doesn't want. He shoves himself into a metal box and faces traffic, burning fuel and patience, just to reach another concrete box where he will spend eight, ten hours performing tasks that, most of the time, have no intrinsic meaning for his soul.

Why does he do this? To earn the money necessary to pay for the metal box and the concrete box.

It is a closed loop of circular logic. We work to afford a house we return to too exhausted to enjoy, only to sleep and recover the energy to work again the next day to ensure we won't lose the house. The System created a labyrinth where the prize for reaching the end of the day is simply the permission to start the next.

In this process, something fundamental is lost: the "freeness" of life. The beauty of a sunset, the pleasure of an unhurried conversation, the silence of a forest these things are useless to the System because they are free. What cannot be monetized is treated as a waste of time. If you spend an afternoon just looking at the sea, the world will call you a loafer. But if you spend that same afternoon selling insurance over the phone in a windowless cubicle, you will be called a "productive member of society."

The farce of progress tells us we are better off than our ancestors because we have Wi-Fi and air conditioning. But our ancestors, however harsh their lives were, did not spend their existence fearing a stock market crash or a productivity algorithm. They were not "resources." They were people. They belonged to the land; today, the land belongs to corporations, and we are temporary tenants.

The cost of being alive in modernity is our peace of mind. To keep the flow of capital moving, the System needs you to be an insatiable consumer. And to be an insatiable consumer, you need to be unhappy. Happy, satisfied, and peaceful people don't need to buy new things all the time. They don't need retail therapy to fill the void left by a purposeless job. They don't need status to validate their existence.

Therefore, the System bombards the Modern Worker with messages of insufficiency. "You aren't beautiful enough," "You aren't successful enough," "You don't have the latest gadget." We have created a society where self-esteem is bought in installments. We are paying interest on our own identity.

This financial performance of existence disconnects us from our biological essence. We are animals of flesh and bone, made of stardust and ancient instincts. We were designed for movement, for deep social connection, for the observation of nature. We were not designed to stare at Excel spreadsheets under fluorescent lights. The depression and anxiety plaguing the Panicked Anthill are not glitches in the system; they are perfectly logical responses to an environment that is fundamentally hostile to human nature.

The human body is trying to say something, but we silence it with medication so it can keep operating. "My soul hurts," says the Modern Worker. "Take this pill and get back to the office," responds the System. The goal is not a cure; it is the maintenance of functionality. The machine doesn't care if the cog is sad, as long as it keeps turning.

We need to question the price we are paying. I'm not just talking about money, but the opportunity cost of being human. What did you stop doing because you "didn't have the money"? What did you stop being because you needed to "be someone"? How many dreams were sacrificed on the altar of financial stability—a stability that, as we've seen in recent crises, is an illusion that can vanish overnight?

The System is a fiction we all agree to maintain. Money is a collective myth. Borders are imaginary lines. Corporations are legal concepts with no heart or lungs. The only real thing is your conscious experience. The only real thing is the warmth of the sun on your skin, the taste of food, the weight of the body of the one you love against yours. And yet, we spend most of our time worried about the fictions, neglecting reality.

We are the only species that pays to live here, and we act as if it were a privilege. But the truth is, the planet never sent us a bill. The trees keep bearing fruit without asking for anyone's ID. The sun keeps shining without demanding a public lighting fee. The scarcity that drives us is, for the most part, manufactured. We produce enough food to feed twelve billion people, yet we let millions starve because they don't have the necessary scraps of paper to validate the right to eat.

This is the "farce of progress." We call a system that places profit above life "civilization." We call a process that turns forests into parking lots and human beings into automatons "development."

The price of being alive has become so high that many of us have forgotten how to simply *be*. We are always *doing*. Always running. Always producing. Always consuming. If we stop, the silence scares us, because in the silence we hear the voice of our soul whispering that we are wasting the miracle of consciousness on something profoundly trivial.

The Modern Worker feels this weight in his chest every morning. It is the weight of knowing he is a spare part in a machine that doesn't love him. It is the exhaustion of a performance that never ends. The system wants you to believe the solution is to earn more money, climb another rung, buy a bigger house. But that is just raising the stakes in a rigged game. The more you have, the more you owe the System in terms of maintenance, insurance, taxes, and worries. You don't own things; things own you.

In the end, the System feeds on our fear. The fear of being "nobody." The fear of not having. The fear of being excluded from the anthill. But what if the price is too high? What if a "career" is just a fancy name for the theft of your time? What if "prosperity" is just a more luxurious cage?

Recognizing that we are paying to live is the first step toward liberation. It doesn't mean you should drop everything and move into a cave tomorrow (though for some, that looks increasingly attractive). It means changing your relationship with the game. It means understanding that the System is a tool, not a god. It means beginning to protect your time as the sacred treasure it is.

The greatest tragedy of modern life is not that we die; it is what dies inside of us while we are still alive. Curiosity dies, wonder dies, the capacity to just exist without an economic justification dies. The Modern Worker has become a master at surviving, but illiterate at living.

Look at the sparrow again. He has no savings, no career plan, and no life insurance. And yet, he wakes up singing. He trusts in the abundance of the world. We, with all our intelligence, created a world where trust is impossible and anxiety is the norm.

What are we doing with our time here? Are we truly building something, or are we just digging a hole for others to fill with concrete? The price of being alive should not be your soul. The right to existence should not be a commercial transaction.

As you close this chapter, do not look for a quick fix or an investment guide. Just feel the absurdity. Feel the strangeness of being a cosmic animal that needs a proof of residence to have a place to drop dead. Feel the indignation of knowing your time is being drained by a gear that only wants more from you, never your well-being.

The cage door is still open. The problem is we were taught that the world outside is too dangerous, because out there, there are no financial guarantees. But in here, the only guarantee we have is that we will be spent until the very end. And when the last bill is paid and the last shift is served, what will be left of you? What will remain of that child who once looked at the world and saw not a market, but a playground?

The system wants you to keep buying the bandages. It doesn't want you to realize that the wound is caused by the very life it forces you to lead. The price of being alive is high, yes. But the greatest loss is paying that price and never actually getting to live.

Take a deep breath. That air entering your lungs right now? It is still free. The beating of your heart? It doesn't belong to your boss. The thought crossing your mind this instant? The System cannot tax it. Start there. Start reclaiming the territories of your life that haven't been subdivided yet. The revolution doesn't start in the streets; it starts when the Modern Worker looks at the bill of existence and says: "I am more than what I produce."

You are not a battery. You are not a resource. You are the miracle of life observing itself. And that, my friend, is something no money in the world can buy and no debt can erase. The game is a farce, and the only way to win is to stop taking the rules so seriously. The sun will rise tomorrow, regardless of the stock market close. And it will shine for you, for free, as it always has. The question is: will you be too busy paying to live, or will you finally open the window to receive what is already yours?

PART 2

The Prison of Glass and Algorithms

CHAPTER 4

The Golden Cage of Convenience

Imagine, for a moment, the prisons of old. Walls of damp stone, bars of solid iron, the metallic clank of keys turning in heavy locks, and the watchful gaze of armed guards. That was a rudimentary form of control. It was honest, in a way. You knew you were a prisoner. You felt the cold of the cell and the roughness of the chains. The System, in its infancy, was still crude, unsophisticated. It believed that to dominate the human animal, it had to inflict physical pain and spatial restriction.

But time passed. The System evolved. It realized that brute force breeds resistance, and resistance breeds revolution. If you squeeze a man's throat too hard, he will fight for his last breath. But if you offer him a down pillow, a remote control, and the promise that he will never have to stand up for anything again, he will hand over his soul voluntarily.

Welcome to your cell, Modern Worker. It is climate-controlled, has high-speed Wi-Fi, and the walls are decorated with prints you bought during an online flash sale. You call it "home." The System calls it an optimized retention unit.

The Golden Cage is not made of metal; it is woven from the invisible threads of **convenience**.

Observe your daily life. What once required effort, movement, and interaction with the physical world has now been reduced to a subtle flick of your thumb over a glass surface. Are you hungry? You don't need to hunt, plant, or even walk to the market. The System has created algorithms that know what you want to eat before your stomach even growls. With three taps, a stranger—another Modern Worker, perhaps in an even more precarious position within the gears—crosses the city to deliver hot food to your door. You don't have to speak to anyone. You don't have to look into the eyes of the person who prepared the meal. The transaction is aseptic, efficient, and terribly lonely.

This is the first bar of your cage: the **atrophy of autonomy**.

The System wants you to be incapable of surviving without it. It sells ease as if it were freedom, but the truth is the opposite. The more convenient your life becomes, the more dependent you are on the infrastructure that enslaves you. You no longer know how to navigate without a GPS. You don't know how to cook without a video tutorial. You don't know how to handle silence without a podcast filling the vacuum. You have become a master of technology, but you are illiterate at living.

Progress—that farce the System so relentlessly propagates—is measured by how much friction we can eliminate from our lives. "Less friction!" shout the Silicon Valley engineers. "More agility!" demand the CEOs. Yet, friction is exactly what gives us traction. It is in the effort of overcoming a difficulty that human character is forged. When everything is easy, nothing has weight. And when nothing has weight, you drift wherever the wind of the algorithm blows.

Consider distraction. In the past, tyrants banned books. Today, the System does something far more perverse: it gives us all the books, all the movies, all the music, and all the cat videos in the world at once. It floods your senses until your capacity for focus is reduced to that of a common fly.

You sit down to read something profound, to think about your life, to perhaps plan your escape. But then, the phone vibrates. A notification. A "like" from someone you barely know. An urgent news story about something that will not change your destiny in the slightest. A ten-second video that makes your brain release a crumb of dopamine. Before you know it, you've spent two hours scrolling.

The System no longer needs armed guards because it has turned you into your own jailer. The algorithm is the invisible whip that keeps your attention turned toward nothingness, while your real life—the one made of time and breath—pours down the drain. You are a battery for the system, and your attention is the voltage that keeps it running. Every second you spend staring at the screen is a second you are not looking at your own prison.

"But I am free!" you say, while adjusting the brightness on your latest-generation smartphone. "I choose what to buy, I choose what to watch, I choose where to work."

Are you sure?

Choosing between ten brands of detergent produced by two major corporations is not freedom of choice; it is the **illusion of agency**. Choosing which series to binge-watch over the weekend while your body craves sunlight and movement is not leisure; it is anesthesia. The System is a sophisticated plantation owner that swapped the whipping post for chronic fatigue and the pillory for performance anxiety.

The Golden Cage is designed so that you never feel the urge to leave. Why would you? It's hard out there. Out there, you have to deal with the weather, with real people and their complexities, with the uncertainty of existence. Inside the cage, everything is guaranteed—as long as you keep paying the subscription. And to pay the subscription, you need to produce. To produce, you must sacrifice your time. And your time is the only thing you truly possess before you return to the dust.

What are we doing, Modern Worker? We are trading the gold of our existence for the brass of convenience.

The System has convinced us that happiness is a state of absolute comfort. But absolute comfort is the state of a corpse. Life is uncomfortable. Life is uncertain. Life demands that you leave the burrow, that you feel the chill down your spine, that you lose your way and have to find your own path back. By outsourcing our orientation to algorithms and our survival to delivery services, we are handing over the keys to our free will.

Look around you now. See the objects that surround you. How many of them were bought to fill a void that the System itself created? It makes you feel insufficient, ugly, outdated, or lonely through the screens, and then offers you the "convenience" of buying the solution in one click. It is the perfect business model: create the problem and sell the bandage, all without you having to leave the couch.

The Prison of Glass and Algorithms is silent. There are no screams of pain, only the constant hum of servers and the incessant click-click of keyboards. We are eight billion people living in individual cells, connected by fiber optic cables but disconnected from our own animal essence. We forgot the smell of the earth after rain because we are too busy choosing the ideal filter for a photo of the window. We forgot the sound of a friend's voice because it's more convenient to send a voice note at 2x speed.

The System fears only one thing: the moment you decide that convenience is not worth the price of your soul. It fears the day the Modern Worker looks at the comfort of their cage and feels nauseated. Because at that moment, the cage loses its luster. The gold is revealed as cheap paint peeling over iron bars.

You were not made to be a data processor. You did not evolve for eons to be a passive consumer of cheap entertainment. You are a biological miracle, a cosmic explorer, a being capable of creating beauty and meaning out of chaos. But the System doesn't want beauty; it wants productivity. It doesn't want meaning; it wants consumption.

The Golden Cage of Convenience is the greatest farce of

progress because it removes the need for us to be human. It transforms us into soft gears, lubricated by instant pleasures, ready to be replaced when the wear becomes excessive.

How do you escape a cage that has no visible bars?

It isn't by breaking windows or tearing down walls. The escape begins the moment you choose the harder path just because it is yours. It begins when you turn off the screen and stare into the void until it starts talking to you. It begins when you decide you prefer the uncertainty of freedom to the comfort of servitude.

The silent revolution of this century will not be fought with weapons, but with the refusal to be convenient. It is the choice to walk instead of drive. To cook instead of order. To read a book instead of scrolling the feed. To look at the sky instead of the digital map.

The System will try to bring you back. It will send personalized notifications. It will offer exclusive discounts. It will create new fears so that you seek new securities. It will tell you that you are falling behind, that the world is changing, and that you need to adapt to survive.

But you have survived things much worse than a lack of Wi-Fi. You are the apex of a lineage of survivors who faced predators, ice ages, and plagues without the help of a delivery app. The strength you seek is not in the next software update; it is in the blood running through your veins—blood that belongs to no corporation.

The Modern Worker needs to awaken to the fact that their "career," their material "achievements," and their "ease of life" are merely layers of varnish on their cell door. Real life is happening out there, in the unpredictable, dirty, and wonderful world that the System tries to hide from you with high-definition screens.

The cage door is open. It always has been. The System just bet that you would be too distracted by the glitter of the gold to notice. It bet that you would prefer the safety of the prison to the responsibility of being free.

The question that remains, as the blue light of your device illuminates your face, is simple:

How much longer will you keep paying rent to live in your own captivity?

The sun is rising out there. And, believe me, it is much sharper than any 4K screen. It is time to stop being a spare part. It is time to be human again, with all the discomfort and all the glory that it carries. Leave the cage. The world misses you.

CHAPTER 5

The Filter of Dissatisfaction

You wake up. Before your feet even touch the cold floor, before the first conscious thought about the day ahead takes shape, your hand fumbles for the nightstand. It's a Pavlovian reflex. The smartphone's blue glow hits your pupils, still dilated from sleep, and there it is: you have just invited the entire world to lie down in bed with you.

In that exact moment, the Modern Worker commits the first mistake of the day. You enter a gladiatorial arena where the weapons are saturation filters and the reward is a validation that evaporates in seconds. Before you even know if you are okay, you need to know how everyone else is pretending to be.

Welcome to the most claustrophobic chapter of our journey.

Welcome to the "Filter of Dissatisfaction".

The Curation of the Lie

What you see on that screen is not life. It is an edited trailer, with an epic soundtrack and fast cuts, of an existence that, up close, is just as mundane and full of bills as yours. But your brain—that marvelous organ that evolved to protect us from predators on the savannah and not from algorithms in Silicon Valley—does not understand the distinction.

You look at the photo of that influencer in Bali, sipping a green juice with flawless skin, and instantly your instant coffee tastes like sand. You look at the "hustle culture" entrepreneur posting about his eleventh million before 6:00 AM, and your job—the one that keeps a roof over your head—suddenly turns into a prison sentence.

The System loves this. In fact, the System designed this.

The primary function of social networks is not to connect people; it is to create abysses. Connecting people is the side effect that keeps us addicted, but the abyss is the real product. It is the gap between who you are and the digital projection of who you think you should be. And it is in this space, in this vacuum of inadequacy, that Capitalism builds its shopping centers and its aesthetic clinics.

The Broken Mirror

Imagine you walk into a store to buy a mirror. When you get home and hang it on the wall, you notice something strange: it doesn't reflect you. It reflects a version of you that is 20% thinner, 30% wealthier, and 100% happier. At first, you are enchanted. But every time you step away from the mirror and look at your own arms, your own stomach, your own bank account, you feel a deep loathing. You begin to hate reality because it doesn't match the reflection.

Social media is that broken mirror.

We have stopped living experiences and started "curating" content. The Modern Worker no longer goes to a concert to hear the music; he goes to prove to others that he was there. He doesn't savor the plate of food; he sacrifices it at the altar of the perfect angle until the food is cold and the soul is hungry.

We have turned our existence into a constant performance. We are actors, directors, and editors of a play that no one really watches closely, because every other spectator is too busy rehearsing their own lines. The result? A profound loneliness in a crowded room.

The System, that invisible jailer, watches it all from the front row. It knows that as long as you are busy trying to "win" on Instagram, you won't have the energy to question why you are working 60 hours a week on something that makes no sense. Digital dissatisfaction is the perfect fuel for industrial productivity.

The Economy of Inadequacy

Think with me: what would happen to the global economy if, tomorrow, all eight billion human beings woke up perfectly satisfied with who they are and what they have?

The stock market would collapse before lunch. The fashion industry would die. Cosmetic companies would evaporate. Luxury gyms, status cars, the annual release of phones that do exactly the same thing as the previous model—all of it would cease to exist.

The System does not want you to heal. It needs you to be a "soft gear," someone who can be molded by the pressure of comparison. A satisfied individual is a net loss for the Machine. Therefore, the algorithm is programmed to show you exactly what you do not have. It maps your insecurities with the precision of a surgeon and pokes them with the glow of a notification.

Do you feel ugly? Here are ten photos of symmetrical faces edited with artificial intelligence. Do you feel poor? Here is a video of a teenager unboxing a Lamborghini. Do you feel alone? Look at your ex-boyfriend toasting at a party surrounded by smiling "friends."

The Filter of Dissatisfaction ensures that your dopamine levels are always low enough that you need a "dose" of consumption to feel human again. You buy a new pair of sneakers not because you need to walk, but because you need that momentary relief of feeling that, for a few minutes, you belong to the world of the successful.

The Death of the Present Moment

There was a time, before the Prison of Glass, when things just happened. A sunset was an event between you and the horizon. A family dinner was a tangle of voices, laughter, and the smell of food. If no one took a photo, the event was still real. It was kept in the memory—that sacred, imprecise place where colors take on the tone of emotion.

Today, if it isn't in the feed, it didn't happen.

The Modern Worker has become illiterate at living in the present. He is always one step ahead, thinking of the caption, or one step behind, checking the likes. The real experience is mediated by a lens. We see life through a 6-inch rectangular frame.

This "Farce of Progress" has convinced us that documenting life is more important than living it. We have created immense digital archives of moments we never truly tasted. We are librarians of an empty history.

And what does this constant mediation do to our soul? It empties it. Because the soul does not feed on pixels. The soul feeds on presence, touch, smell, and silence. But silence generates no engagement. Presence cannot be monetized by the Algorithm. So, the System pushes us toward noise, toward stridency, toward the eternal "look at me."

The Anatomy of the Void

You know that void you feel in your chest at two in the morning, after spending hours endlessly scrolling? That feeling that you are missing something important, that the party of life is happening somewhere else and you weren't invited?

This has a name: **"Fear Of Missing Out"** (FOMO). But I prefer to call it "The Pain of the Spare Part." It is the moment when your biological self screams to your digital self that you are starving for reality.

The System tries to convince you that this void is a manufacturing defect of yours. It gives you diagnoses, sells you happiness pills, and offers you "mindfulness" courses so you can endure a little more anxiety. But this void is not an error. It is a sign of health. It is your human nature resisting domestication by the algorithm.

We were designed to look into eyes, not at screens. We were designed to live in tribes of 150 people where everyone knows each other, not in global villages of billions where no one cares. The Filter of Dissatisfaction tries to squeeze a giant—the human spirit—into a digital shoebox. Of course it's going to hurt.

Breaking the Lens

So, what do we do? How can the Modern Worker escape this trap of mirrors?

The answer is simple, but it is the hardest thing you will try to do this decade: **you must start being "useless" to the System**.

Being useless to the System means having hobbies that don't produce money. It means spending entire afternoons without posting a single photo. It means looking at your reflection in the mirror in the morning the real one, with dark circles and messy hair—and not feeling the immediate need to correct it.

We need to understand that technological progress has given us incredible tools, but these tools came with a price: our peace of mind. The farce of progress is believing that the more "connected" we are, the more human we become. The truth is the opposite. With every filter we apply to our photos, we remove a layer of our truth.

The Filter of Dissatisfaction only loses power when you stop looking sideways. When you realize that the other person's life, however bright it seems on the screen, is just a snippet. And snippets have no depth. Snippets have no flesh.

The Invitation to Discomfort

At this point in the reading, you must be feeling an impulse. Maybe you want to close this book and check your notifications. Maybe you are thinking: "But I need social media for my work, for my career."

The System is a master at using necessity as a leash. It mixes your survival with your vanity so you cannot separate one from the other. But here is a secret: you can be a competent professional without being a slave to the digital storefront. You can be a cosmic animal without needing approval in the form of a little heart.

The Prison of Glass and Algorithms is made of a very fragile material: your attention. If you withdraw your attention, the glass blurs, the algorithm starves, and the cell disappears.

The challenge I leave you with, Modern Worker, as we close this chapter, is the exercise of invisibility. Try to live something wonderful today and tell no one. Don't post it. Don't photograph it. Just feel it. Let the experience die with you, inside you, like a precious secret between you and existence.

You will find that without the filter of comparison, reality—with all its imperfections, its pains, and its grime—is infinitely more vibrant than any high-definition image.

The sun that rises outside doesn't need "likes" to shine. And neither do you. It is time to stop paying rent on a life that isn't yours. It is time to clear the lens and see the world as it is: a chaotic, unpredictable, and absolutely wonderful place that fits into no algorithm.

Step out of the display case. Real life is happening on the sidewalk, and it misses you.

CHAPTER 6

The Cry of the Sou

Have you ever felt that sudden tightening in your chest, in the middle of a Tuesday afternoon, for no apparent reason? It isn't a heart attack, though it feels as if your heart is trying to escape your ribcage. It isn't a lack of air, though the oxygen in the air-conditioned room suddenly seems thinner. It is a restlessness that has no name in performance reviews—a dissonant vibration that ripples through your body while you stare at an Excel spreadsheet or wait for the coffee to finish brewing in the office breakroom.

The System has a name for this. It calls it a disorder. It calls it a chemical imbalance. It labels you as a "Human Resource" with a manufacturing defect and promptly suggests you seek a repair. After all, a Spare Part that doesn't function with mathematical precision is a loss for the Machine. The System wants you to believe that your anguish is an individual error—a glitch in your internal gears that can, and should, be silenced with a colorful pill, a ten-minute meditation app, or a spiritual retreat on the next long weekend.

But I want to propose a different perspective to you, Modern Worker. What if this void—this anxiety gnawing at the edges of your day—is not a defect? What if it is, in fact, the only sane thing about you?

Imagine you are a lion. A Biological Miracle, designed by millions of years of evolution to hunt, to run under the sun, to smell the damp earth, and to live in a complex, fierce community. Now, imagine this lion is placed in a two-by-two-meter glass cage, fed processed kibble, and forced to watch videos of other lions running on a high-definition screen. After a few months, the lion begins to pace back and forth, to snarl at nothing, to lick its own paws until they bleed.

The zoologist would say the lion is sick. But the sickness is not in the lion; the sickness is the cage.

The Cry of the Soul is the snarl of the lion that still lives inside you. You are a Cosmic Animal that has been domesticated to become a Passive Consumer. You evolved to observe the stars and decipher the rhythms of the tides, yet today you spend your intellect processing data that means nothing to your biological survival, only to feed an algorithm that doesn't even know you exist. Your body—this temple of ultra-sophisticated sensors—is being used merely as a tripod to carry your head from one video meeting to another.

What we call an "existential crisis" is, in truth, a biological alarm system. It is your soul pounding on the walls of this Glass Prison, screaming that you were not born to be a Battery for the System. This discomfort you feel when you realize your life has turned into an infinite sequence of bills and notifications is proof that you are still alive. Apathy would be the final death. Suffering, as ironic as it may seem, is the sign that your humanity is still resisting.

We have become Illiterate at Living because we traded depth for speed. The System convinced us that peace is a product that can be bought on the "self-help" shelf, when, in reality, peace is the byproduct of a life aligned with our nature. But how can one align with nature when your natural habitat has been replaced by a concrete jungle, push notifications, and blue light?

Observe how the Invisible Jailer operates: he creates the disease and then sells the cure. He drains you of every last drop of vital energy and then offers you an energy drink so you can work two more hours. He destroys your sense of community and then sells you a social network so you can feel an artificial, hollow connection. He disconnects you from your purpose and then offers you a course on "how to find your passion" for just twelve easy installments on your credit card.

The Cry of the Soul is a protest against this farce. It is the part of you that refuses to be merely a "Productive Member of Society" if that means ceasing to be a human being.

When anxiety knocks on your door today, do not try to drive it away immediately as if it were a virus. Sit with it. Listen to what it has to say. Often, it is only whispering: "This is not what I should be doing." It is reminding you that time is the only real currency, and you are wasting it on a transaction where the profit is never yours.

The Jailer himself is the one who believes silence is dangerous. This is why we fill every second of our lives with noise. Earphones on the subway, podcasts while we wash the dishes, the radio on in the car. We are terrified of what silence might reveal to us. We fear that in the vacuum of external noise, the Cry of the Soul will become deafening. And it will. It will tell you that that promotion won't fulfill you. That the new car won't cure the loneliness. That the validation of strangers on the internet is a food that never sates the hunger to be truly seen.

You are not a system error, Temporary Tenant of existence. You are a walking biological protest. Your pain is the compass pointing to where your freedom was buried.

The challenge now is not to silence the cry, but to have the courage to follow it. It is to understand that this pressure in your chest is not a signal to speed up and produce more to "win at life," but rather an imperative command to stop. To look around. To realize that the cage door is ajar and that the jailer only has power as long as you believe in the farce of progress he sells.

Listen to the cry. It is not your enemy. It is the sound of your soul trying to wake you up before the final breath arrives and you realize you spent your entire life being a Soft Gear in a machine that, the second you stop spinning, will simply replace you with another part—newer, cheaper, and quieter.

Your soul is screaming because it refuses to die in silence. And that, my dear Modern Worker, is the most beautiful thing about you.

PART 3

The Market of Insecurity

CHAPTER 7

Connected and Lonely

Look to your side right now. If you are on the subway, in a café, or in a doctor's waiting room, what do you see? A collection of bowed necks. A row of human beings—biological miracles that took millions of years to develop an upright posture—now voluntarily folded over small rectangles of glowing glass. We are all physically present, but our minds have been hijacked. We are "connected."

But please, do not confuse connection with "presence".

The System—that sophisticated plantation owner governing our days—has pulled off the greatest masterstroke in human history: it convinced us that being in touch with everything means not being alone with anything. It traded the depth of the village for the infinite, yet shallow, extension of the network. And you, the Modern Worker, accepted the trade without reading the fine print. The result? You have never been so surrounded by voices, yet you have never felt so profoundly lonely.

In the past, humans gathered around the fire. The fire warmed the body, and stories warmed the soul. There was silence between sentences, and that silence was shared. Today, the blue glow of screens is our new fire, but it has a perverse property: it illuminates the face but does not warm the chest. It merely projects the shadow of our own inadequacy against the wall of the digital cave.

You have become what I call the "Slave of the Digital Storefront." Your life is no longer something you experience, but something you edit. You are the actor, the director, and the editor of a hollow story that you publish for people who are too busy editing their own lies to pay attention to your truth. The System loves this. Do you know why? Because people seeking external validation are the perfect consumers. Your loneliness is the fuel that keeps the Gears turning. If you were at peace with yourself, sitting on a park bench just watching the wind in the trees, you wouldn't be clicking, you wouldn't be buying, and above all, you wouldn't be feeding the Algorithm.

Modern connectivity is a banquet of empty calories. You consume hundreds of interactions a day—likes, comments, views—and yet you end the night with a devastating spiritual hunger. It is like drinking saltwater to quench your thirst; the more you drink, the more dehydrated you become. The System turned friendship into a metric. It turned affection into a "like" button. And it turned your biological need to belong to a group into a constant anxiety of being excluded from the feed.

We have lost the basic wisdom of "just being".

Think of your inner cosmic animal. It was not designed to process the lives of five thousand "friends." It was designed to recognize the smell of damp earth, to feel the rhythm of the seasons, and to trust the tight circle of its tribe. When you expand that circle to the digital infinite, your capacity for real connection dilutes until it vanishes. You know what your former schoolmate ate for lunch in Paris, but you don't know the name of the neighbor living next door. You send a heart "emoji" to a stranger, but you cannot hold the gaze of someone you love for more than thirty seconds without feeling the nervous impulse to check your notifications.

The System is an invisible jailer that uses your desire for connection against you. It knows that loneliness hurts. It knows that isolation is the greatest torture for a social animal. So, it offers the palliative: "Here, take this device. With it, you will never be alone again." But it is a lie. What it gives you is a noisy crowd that prevents you from hearing your own voice. It gives you a connectivity that isolates you from reality.

You, the Master of Technology, have become illiterate at living in the present. The present moment has become an obstacle between you and the next post. If you see a marvelous sunset, your first reaction isn't to take a deep breath and feel the grandeur of the universe. It is to fumble in your pocket for your phone. You need to capture, filter, and post. If the sunset isn't validated by strangers, did it really happen? For the Modern Worker, the answer is, tragically, no. If there was no digital footprint, the experience has no market value. And the System only cares about what has market value.

We traded community for an audience.

In a community, you are seen with all your flaws, scars, and eccentricities. You are accepted for your humanity. In an audience, you must perform. You must be a **Soft Gear**, without edges, perfectly polished for others' consumption. The performance is exhausting. That is why you feel so tired even when you spend the day sitting down. Maintaining the farce of a perfect life on the feed requires a vital energy that should be used for, well, living.

Modern loneliness is a direct byproduct of this performance. You feel alone because the person people "love" online isn't you. It is the character you created. And deep down, your soul knows it. It screams because it perceives that you are building a sandcastle while the tide of reality is rising. You have a thousand followers, but no one to help you move the couch or to hold your hand in a moment of real grief. You have WhatsApp groups that never stop pinging, but the silence inside your home is deafening.

What are we doing, after all? We are sacrificing the real for the virtual, the tangible for the pixelated. We are trading the warmth of an embrace for the coldness of a retina display. And we call this progress. We call this being at the forefront of evolution.

But the wisdom of "just being" does not require a Wi-Fi signal. It requires courage. The courage to disconnect. The courage to face the void that appears when the screen goes black. The System is terrified of that void, because it is in the void that you begin to think. It is in the silence that you begin to realize the golden cage has no lock. It is in the absence of distractions that you reconnect with your biological animal, with your real needs for touch, for sight, for presence.

You are not a data processor. You are not a human resource to be mined by attention algorithms. You are a miracle of consciousness who has been deceived by an "Invisible Jailer". He convinced you that the whole world fits in the palm of your hand, but by closing your hand around that device, you let go of the hand of life.

The farce of connectivity is that it keeps us close enough to compare ourselves, but far enough not to help each other. The Algorithm profits from your envy, from your fear of missing out (the notorious FOMO), and from your desperate need not to be forgotten. But the truth is that in the grand theater of the System, we are all spare parts. If you stop posting today, the feed will continue tomorrow as if you never existed. The machine does not love you. It merely processes you.

The cure for this connected loneliness is not found in a new app or a faster phone model. It lies in reclaiming the wisdom of boundaries. It lies in understanding that your attention is your most precious asset—and you are giving it away for free to billionaires who sell it to advertisers.

Imagine if you invested half the time you spend looking at the filtered photos of strangers into looking inside yourself. Imagine if you swapped ten minutes of scrolling for ten minutes of real conversation, with no phones at the table, with someone you love. The world wouldn't change, but **your** world would change. The pressure in your chest would begin to yield. The void would begin to be filled not by content, but by meaning.

We are living the paradox of hyper-connection: we have never talked so much and never said so little. We have never had so many "contacts" and never been so helpless. The Modern Worker is a castaway in an ocean of information, dying of thirst for meaning.

The System wants you to keep swimming frantically, trying to reach the next island of digital validation. I invite you to simply stop swimming. Let yourself float for a moment. Feel the real water around your real body. Turn off the signal. Silence the notifications. Look at the person in front of you, or look in the mirror, and recognize the human being who is there, behind the filters, behind the metrics, behind the exhaustion.

The wisdom of "just being" is the greatest act of rebellion you can practice today. In a world that demands you be everywhere at once, having the courage to be only here, now, is your only chance at freedom. You were not made to be a battery for the system. You were made to be the protagonist of your own sensory and emotional experience.

Connected and lonely? Perhaps. But only as long as you believe the network is the world. The world, the real one, is out there, waiting for you to lift your head and see it. No cameras. No filters. Just you and the mystery of existence.

Stop being a Soft Gear for a moment. Let the Algorithm starve. Reclaim your solitude, for only those who know how to be alone can truly be with another. Connectivity gave us distant neighbors and intimate strangers, but presence gives us back to ourselves.

What are we doing? We are losing life while trying to record it. We are losing love while trying to measure it. We are losing peace while trying to sell it.

It is time to disconnect to finally find the way home. And home, my dear Modern Worker, was never an IP address. Home is the place where you don't need Wi-Fi to feel whole.

CHAPTER 8

The Bandage Industry

Have you ever felt that sudden discomfort in your chest the moment you turn off your alarm? It's not a physical pain—the kind a cardiologist could explain with charts and blood tests. It's something subtler, a sort of itch on the soul, a persistent whisper telling you that something is deeply wrong. The System—that invisible jailer you've learned to call a "lifestyle" hears that whisper even before you do. And it already has the solution ready, wrapped in biodegradable plastic and available in twelve easy installments on your credit card.

Welcome to the "Bandage Industry".

The Modern Worker is, by definition, a wounded creature. You are wounded by the routine that crushes you, by the air conditioning that dries out your skin, and by the blue light that melts your ability to concentrate. You are wounded by the constant comparison in the digital storefront, where the lives of others look like a Hollywood movie while yours feels like a documentary about exhaustion. But here is the secret that keeps the gears turning: "The System does not want you to hea". If you heal, you become a terrible consumer.

A happy man, satisfied and at peace with what he sees in the mirror, is a technical bankruptcy for the market. Resolved people don't buy sports cars to overcompensate for a midlife crisis. People who feel whole don't need "ten steps to happiness" or vitamin supplements that promise the energy that work stole from them. The modern economy is a house of cards built upon the swamp of your insecurity.

The System operates like a perverse pharmacist who,

49

surreptitiously, puts drops of poison in your morning coffee only to sell you the antidote in the afternoon. But the antidote is never a cure; it is merely a colorful bandage. Its purpose is to staunch the bleeding just long enough for you to get back to your workstation and produce more wealth for those who sell the poison.

Look around you, dear Cosmic Animal. What are "fifteen-day vacations" if not a bandage for an entire year of servitude? You spend eleven and a half months accumulating stress, cortisol, and resentment, only to "recharge your batteries" at a resort where you pay the equivalent of three months' salary to drink cocktails with colorful umbrellas. You aren't resting; you are merely undergoing maintenance. You are a "Spare Part" that needs lubrication so the engine doesn't seize. As soon as the vacation bandage falls off, the wound is still there—raw, pulsing, and waiting for Monday.

And what can be said of the "wellness" industry? It has become a multi-billion dollar market. We have apps that teach us to meditate for ten minutes so we can endure ten hours of corporate abuse. We have spiritual retreats that cost a fortune, where you can be "authentic" in a controlled environment, provided you post a photo of your enlightenment on Instagram. This is the farce at its peak: we have turned the search for the soul into just another consumer item. The System took your existential anguish—which should have been the engine of your liberation—and turned it into a market niche.

You, the Modern Worker, have become a master at layering bandages. When anxiety strikes, you apply the bandage of cheap entertainment, wasting hours in an infinite scroll of short videos that leave nothing behind but a trail of cheap dopamine in your brain. When loneliness bites, you use the bandage of digital validation, seeking in the "likes" of strangers the human warmth that the asphalt of the cold city denied you. When the void of purpose becomes unbearable, you buy something new. A gadget, a garment, a new "high-performance" course.

But the skin beneath the bandage is rotting.

The Bandage Industry survives by maintaining your pain at a bearable level. If the pain is too great, you break and stop producing—which is bad for profit. If the pain disappears, you realize you don't need any of this—which is fatal for profit. The perfect balance for the System is to keep you in a state of "near-sickness": functional enough to operate the machine, but miserable enough to need to buy the next temporary fix.

What are we doing, after all? We are decorating the walls of our prison with advertisements for freedom. We are trying to heal a structural wound with superficial solutions. The Modern Worker is a Castaway in an ocean of information who would rather drink saltwater than admit that the ship they are on never had a destination.

The truth is that the cure cannot be bought, and that is why it is so dangerous. The cure for the farce of progress is not in adding something to your life—more money, more success, more followers. The cure lies in subtraction. It lies in ripping off all those expensive bandages and looking at the raw wound. Yes, it will hurt. It will bleed. You will realize that the wound is not a "defect" of yours, but a perfectly healthy reaction to a sick environment.

Your anxiety is not a programming error; it is your biological system screaming that you were not made to be a battery for the system. Your exhaustion is not a lack of vitamins; it is your soul handing in its resignation from a job that makes no sense.

The System wants you to keep buying the bandages because, as long as you are busy changing the dressing, you will never have time to ask who stabbed you in the first place. It is time to stop being a passive consumer of your own misery. It is time to understand that every bandage you buy is one more brick in the wall that separates you from yourself.

The next time you feel the void, do not run to the store, whether physical or digital. Don't turn on the TV. Don't open the app. Sit with your wound. Let it speak. In the silence that follows the tearing of the bandage, you might finally hear what your heart—that eternal cosmic explorer—has been trying to tell you since day one: you are not a gear. And no commodity in the world can cure the pain of pretending that you are.

CHAPTER 9

The Myth of Infinite Growth

Look around you. Not at the objects you possess, but at the logic that placed them there. There is a word that has become the silent religion of our time, a dogma so omnipresent that we rarely stop to question its sanity: "Growth".

In biology, endless growth has a very specific name. We call it "cancer". An organism that decides to ignore its host's limits, that consumes resources without stopping and multiplies wildly, ends up destroying the very foundation that sustains it. However, the System—that sophisticated plantation owner we built—has convinced us that in the economy and in personal life, if you aren't growing, you are dying.

The Myth of Infinite Growth is the greatest piece of fiction ever written by humanity, and you, the Modern Worker, are the exhausted protagonist of this story.

Think of the Gross Domestic Product the famous GDP. It is the heartbeat of the Machine. If a nation's GDP grows by 3% a year, economists pop champagne. But have you ever stopped to do the math behind this euphoria? A growth of 3% per year means the economy must double in size every 24 years. In a century, it would need to be twenty times larger. In two centuries, four hundred times larger.

Now, look at the planet. Look at your lungs. Look at the 24 hours of your day. Where, in this finite world of rock, water, and biological tissues, are we going to find space for this constant "double"? The System operates under the illusion that we live on an infinite plane of digital resources, but we are cosmic animals trapped in a biosphere that has edges, that has limits, and that is beginning to crack under the weight of our statistical greed.

You feel this on your skin every Sunday night. The anxiety rising through your esophagus isn't just worry about work; it is the subconscious perception that the gears are demanding from you something you no longer have to give. The System does not accept "enough." "Enough" is the enemy of profit. If you are satisfied with your car, your house, and your appearance, you become useless to the Gears. For the Machine to keep turning, you must be kept in a perpetual state of lack. You need to believe that your current "self" is an obsolete version in urgent need of an upgrade.

We have turned the Modern Worker into a battery for the system, but a battery that can never be fully charged. The System pushes you toward "more": more productivity, more followers, more courses, more achievements. And when you finally reach the top of the mountain they promised you, the mist clears and you realize the mountain was just a step toward an even larger one. It is the hedonic treadmill transformed into public policy.

This farce of progress ignores a fundamental truth: nature works in cycles, not in ascending straight lines. Trees do not grow until they touch the moon; they grow until they reach balance with the soil and the sun, and then they dedicate themselves to flowering, to bearing fruit, to simply **being**. Winter is not a failure of the solar system; it is a necessary period of retraction and rest. But in our culture, rest is seen as a sin. The pause is interpreted as inefficiency.

The result of this obsession is a kind of collective schizophrenia. We are trying to shove an infinite appetite into a finite stomach. We destroy ancient forests to manufacture disposable furniture that lasts three years. We pollute rivers to mine metals that will be used in phones that will be replaced in eighteen months. And we call this "advancement."

But the real cost isn't just in the environment; it's in your soul. When you accept the myth of infinite growth, you abdicate the present. You live in a state of "when." When I am promoted, I'll be happy. When I double my revenue, I'll have peace. When I buy that house, I'll be able to breathe. The problem is that "when" is a finish line the Machine moves five yards forward every time you get close to it.

You are a biological miracle, a cosmic explorer who received a limited amount of time on this grain of blue dust. Spending this journey trying to satisfy the insatiable hunger of an economic algorithm is the greatest tragedy of our era. The System wants you to fear stagnation, but stagnation is often just peace under another name.

There comes a moment when the only sane attitude is conscious imbalance. It is looking at the proposal of growth and saying: "No, thank you. I already have enough." It is understanding that the most beautiful tree in the forest is not the one that grew the fastest, but the one that managed to grow the deepest roots.

The farce of progress tells us that the future must always be greater than the past. Wisdom, however, tells us that the future will only be possible if we learn the art of being smaller, slower, and much more human. The myth is breaking. You can hear the cracks in the economy, in the climate, and in your own chronic fatigue. The question is no longer how we will keep growing, but what we will do when the illusion finally collapses and we realize that the only thing that truly needed to grow was our capacity to love what we already have.

PART 4

Leaving the Game

CHAPTER 10

Recognizing the Farce

Have you ever stopped to observe the bluish glow of a city at night, from the height of a lookout point or an airplane window? It is a mesmerizing sight. Trails of red and white lights winding through arteries of asphalt, buildings pulsing with the electricity of thousands of lives stacked together. From a distance, it looks like a perfect choreography, a triumph of engineering and human will. But if you zoom in—if you descend to the sidewalk level and look into the eyes of those passing by—the choreography reveals itself as a spasm. The triumph reveals itself as a silent panic.

Right now, the Modern World—that Actor, Director, and Editor of your reality—is trying to sell you the idea that you are "behind." Behind on a deadline, behind on a goal, behind the success of someone you saw on Instagram while you were using the bathroom. The System survives on one basic premise: that what you are now is not enough, and what you have now is merely a draft of what you should have.

But here is the secret the gears try to drown out with the noise of notifications: the game isn't hard to win because you are incapable. The game is impossible to win because the rules were designed so that "winning" is a finish line that recedes every time you take a step.

Recognizing the farce is not an act of cynicism. It is an act of liberation. It is the moment when the Modern Worker—that exhausted protagonist—stops looking at the script they were given and realizes the stage is made of cardboard, the walls are projections, and the audience is too busy looking at their own scripts to notice if he missed a line.

The Architecture of the Absurd

Think about your routine. Not the idealized routine you post on social media, but your naked routine. You wake up to a sound your brain interprets as a danger signal—the alarm. Your body enters a state of alert. You ingest caffeine to silence the biological signs of fatigue your nervous system is screaming. You dress to project an image of competence and conformity. You enter a metal or plastic box to travel to another concrete box, where you will spend the best hours of your day—the most beautiful sunlight—trading your life force for digital numbers in a bank account.

Why do we do this? The standard answer is "survival." But look around. Are we really just surviving? If it were just survival, we wouldn't need luxury cars to get to work, or brand-name clothes to sit in meetings, or smartphones that cost months' worth of food to check emails at eleven at night.

We have turned survival into a performance. The System has convinced you, the Biological Miracle, that you are actually a "Human Resource". Note the perversity of the term. A "resource" is something extracted until it is depleted. Coal is a resource. Oil is a resource. You have become the fuel for a machine that doesn't know where it's going, but insists it needs to get there faster and faster.

The farce lies in the arbitrariness of the rules. Why do we work forty, fifty, sixty hours a week? Why is success measured by our ability to accumulate objects that, in ten years, will be trash in a landfill? Why do we accept that anxiety is the fair price to pay for a career?

The answer is so simple it's frightening: because they told us that's how the game works. And we, like good students, stopped questioning the rules and focused only on how to play them better.

The Broken Mirror

There was a moment—maybe it was yesterday, maybe five years ago—when you felt the crack. It was a moment of sudden silence in the middle of the chaos. Maybe you were in a traffic jam, staring at the bumper of the car ahead, and you thought: "Is this it? Is this what my ancestors fought predators and famine for? So I could sit here, listening to a podcast about productivity while my life pours down the drain?"

In that moment, you glimpsed the farce. You saw the Soft Gear of your own will being chewed up by the Machine. The System hates that moment of clarity. That is why it created a multi-billion dollar industry to distract you the moment the crack appears. Feel a void? Buy something. Feel anxiety? Take this. Feel like life has no meaning? Here are ten new series to binge-watch until exhaustion defeats you.

The System is a perverse pharmacist who sells you the poison and then offers the antidote that only numbs the pain, never healing the wound. It needs you to remain Illiterate at Living—someone who knows how to operate spreadsheets and algorithms but doesn't know what to do with a Tuesday afternoon without a Wi-Fi connection.

The Fallacy of "When"

Another pillar of the farce is the carrot dangled in front of the donkey: the fallacy of "when."

- "When I get promoted, I'll have peace."

- "When I pay off the mortgage, I'll travel."

- "When the kids grow up, I'll go back to painting."

- "When I retire, I'll finally live."

The System loves the future because the future does not exist.

The future is a warehouse where you store all your dreams so they don't interfere with your productivity in the present. By projecting happiness to a point further on the horizon, you ensure you never reach it, because the horizon moves with you.

Recognizing the farce is understanding that "when" is a handcuff. The only life you have—the only one that truly belongs to you—is the time between your first and last breath. And the System wants you to spend that time as a Spare Part, being used until the cost of maintenance is higher than the profit you generate.

The New Metric: Peace as Profit

Imagine a company where the bottom line isn't measured in dollars, but in hours of peaceful sleep. Where the ROI (Return on Investment) is measured by how many times you truly laughed with your friends this week. Where "Exponential Growth" refers to your ability to notice the changing seasons or the taste of a ripe fruit.

For the System, this company would be a total failure. It would be stagnation. But for you, the Cosmic Animal miraculously conscious on this planet spinning in the void, it is the only definition of success that makes sense.

Recognizing the farce is changing the currency. Money remains necessary to pay rent and buy food, as we are still temporary tenants in this economic system. But money stops being the master and becomes the servant again. You stop sacrificing your peace for profit and start sacrificing profit for peace.

The Actor Leaving the Stage

Imagine the life you have led until now is a long-running play. You stepped onto the stage on the first day of school and have followed the script ever since. The costume is tight, the makeup is smeared with sweat, and the footlights are blinding your eyes.

Suddenly, you stop in the middle of an important monologue about "quarterly goals" and look at the audience. You realize the audience is empty. There is no one there to judge you. The Director (the System) is backstage screaming orders, but he has no real power over you if you simply refuse to speak the next line.

You drop the script. The sound of paper hitting the wood echoes through the silent theater. You walk to the edge of the stage, jump into the darkness of the pit, and walk toward the exit.

Outside, the air is cold and real. There is no applause, but there are no demands either. There is only the world, vast and indifferent, waiting to be lived instead of performed.

Recognizing the farce is the first step toward leaving the game. And leaving the game is not losing. It is, finally, beginning to live on your own terms, by your own rules, in your own time.

You are not a resource. You are not a consumer. You are not a battery. You are the miracle the machine tries to process. And the moment you recognize that, the machine loses. And you, perhaps for the first time, breathe.

CHAPTER 11

Living by Your Own Rules

You have stepped through the door. The deafening sound of the gears grinding has been left behind, replaced by a silence that, at first, feels terrifying. It is the silence of the desert, where there are no signposts, no bosses evaluating your performance, and no notifications telling you who you should be today. Now, you are the architect of a vacant lot. But beware: the vacuum is the System's favorite place to whisper back. If you do not fill this space with your own rules, the Machine will send an invitation printed on glossy paper, beckoning you to return to your old post as a "Soft Gear".

Living by your own rules is not an act of cheap anarchy; it is an act of biological sovereignty. For decades, you were trained to be a "Human Resource" a lithium-ion battery that Capitalism consumes and discards once the charge drops below twenty percent. To break this cycle, the first step is to understand that most of the "rules" governing your life are not laws of physics— they are merely marketing suggestions masquerading as destiny.

Imagine the System is a restaurant that serves only three dishes: Career Anxiety, Consumption by Comparison, and Premature Exhaustion. For years, you ate what was on the menu because you thought the kitchen was the universe. Living by your own rules is, finally, writing your own menu.

The first rule of your new life must be the Redefinition of Success.

To the System, success is accumulation; to the biological animal you are, success should be autonomy. The Modern Worker spends an entire life trading the "now" for a "later" that never arrives. We accumulate miles for trips we are too tired to take. We accumulate money to pay for medicines that treat diseases caused by the stress of earning that very money. Break this logic. Your new rule must be: *the value of anything is the amount of life you trade for it.* If an object, a position, or a status requires you to sell your peace of mind, the price is too high. Systemic profit is almost always an existential loss.

The second rule is the Reclamation of "Dead Time".

The System hates idleness. To the Machine, a human being at rest is a wasted resource—a part that isn't creating friction. This is why we were conditioned to feel guilt when we aren't "being productive." You open a book and an internal voice asks: "How will this help my resume?" You look at the sunset and feel the urge to photograph it to prove to the Algorithm that you have an interesting life.

Your new rule? Claim the right to be useless to the market. Cultivate hobbies that cannot be monetized. Learn to play an instrument poorly, just for the pleasure of the sound. Walk without a step-counter strapped to your wrist. When you do something that generates no profit, you are declaring independence. You are telling the Sophisticated Plantation Owner that your vital energy is not for sale by the hour.

The third rule is the Geometry of "Enough."

We live in a world designed to keep us in a state of perpetual lack. The System needs you to feel inadequate because satisfied people make terrible consumers. Living by your own rules requires you to define where necessity ends and the farce begins. How big is the house you actually need to be happy? How many pairs of shoes are necessary to walk with dignity? By establishing your own concept of "enough," you snatch the control of your happiness from the System's hands. Freedom is not in having everything, but in not being possessed by what you possess.

Do not be deceived: the world around you will continue to operate under the old norms. You will still see the Panicked Anthill rushing to hit hollow targets. You will still encounter the Exhausted Protagonist in the elevator, flaunting dark circles under their eyes as if they were medals of honor. The difference is that you will no longer be an actor in that play. You will be the director of a one-man film.

Living by your own rules means accepting that, to many, you will appear to be losing the game. They will see your refusal to climb the corporate ladder as failure. They will see your disconnection from social media as irrelevance. They will see your search for peace as a lack of ambition. Let them think what they will. The price of freedom is the misunderstanding of the captives.

You did not evolve for millions of years, surviving ice ages, predators, and plagues, to end your days answering "urgent" emails at ten o'clock on a Sunday night. You are the pinnacle of a biological miracle, a cosmic explorer temporarily housed in a carbon body. The System wants you to forget this so it can process you as data.

By taking command, you discover that life is not a career to be built, but an experience to be moved through. Your rules must serve to protect that experience. Prioritize sleep over the screen. Prioritize the real encounter over digital engagement. Prioritize your mental health over the growth of the GDP.

In the end, when the last breath approaches and the script of this farce reaches its conclusion, you will not regret not having worked more or not having bought the newest model of a car that is now scrap metal. You will look back and thank yourself for having had the courage to be the sole owner of your time.

Because outside the golden cage, life is vast, raw, and magnificent. And, for the first time, it is truly yours.

CHAPTER 12

The Only Real Currency: Time

Stop for a moment. Close your eyes and feel the pulse in your wrist or the rhythmic expansion of your chest. Each beat, each cycle of oxygen entering and leaving, is not just a physiological process; it is the sound of a countdown. The System—that invisible jailer we call the "modern lifestyle"—has trained you to believe that the most valuable currency in the world is the dollar, the euro, or the digital click of a bank transaction. It has convinced the Modern Worker that scarcity is financial.

But the System lied.

The only real currency—the only one that possesses intrinsic value and that can never be recovered once spent—is time. And you, the pinnacle of a biological miracle, have been the target of a silent and continuous robbery from the moment you learned to tell time on a wall clock.

We live in a collective hallucination where we accept trading our vital substance—the precious minutes of our existence—for pieces of paper or numbers on a screen. We made a pact with the Machine: we hand over our sunny mornings, our afternoons of contemplation, and our nights of deep rest in exchange for the permission to continue existing inside the golden cage. The Modern Worker has become illiterate at living in the present, a being who is always "saving" time through technology, only to discover that the saved time was immediately confiscated by a new demand for productivity.

Think of the irony: we are the Master of Technology, yet we

cannot find ten minutes to observe the movement of the clouds without feeling a sting of guilt. That guilt is the Algorithm speaking inside your head. It wants you to feel that time not spent serving the gears is time wasted. But what, after all, is waste?

Is it a waste to sit in silence and feel the warmth of the sun on your skin? Or is it a waste to spend forty hours a week locked in a room with fluorescent lights, processing data for a corporation that would replace you within twenty-four hours if your heart stopped beating?

You are a Spare Part to the System, but you are a unique cosmic explorer to the universe. The tragedy of modernity is that we spend most of our earthly journey acting as if we were immortal in the execution of irrelevant tasks and dying in the pursuit of what truly makes us vibrate.

The System does not love you. The Machine has no feelings for you. It does not care if you saw your child take their first steps or if you had time to say goodbye to those you loved. To the Gears, you are just a battery, a human resource to be exhausted until your voltage drops and you can be discarded in favor of a newer, faster, less inquisitive model.

Spending your time serving something that has no soul is the most refined form of self-flagellation. We are all running, but to where? The progress they sold us is a straight line toward burnout. The Cycle of Exhaustion feeds on your belief that "in the future" you will have time. In the future, when the promotion comes. In the future, when the bills are paid. In the future, when retirement knocks on the door.

But the future is a marketing fiction. The only thing that exists is now — this breath, this thought, this fraction of a second in which you read these words.

When you begin to see time as your only real currency, your

relationship with the world changes. You stop apologizing for not being available. You start saying "no" to meetings that could have been an email and "yes" to aimless walks. You realize that being "useless to the market" on a Tuesday afternoon can be the most revolutionary act of sanity you've ever practiced.

Leaving the game doesn't necessarily mean moving to a cave; it means recognizing that your time is the private property of your soul, not an asset of the company. It means understanding that every hour sold is an hour of life that never returns. And if you are going to sell your life, the price must be much higher than just a salary that barely covers the cost of keeping you functional enough to work again on Monday.

The Modern Worker must wake up to the fact that they are the director and the protagonist of a one-man film. The System's audience may applaud your productivity, but they won't be there when the lights go out. In the end, the only question that will matter won't be "how much did you accumulate?" but rather "who did you become while the clock was ticking?"

Do not let the farce of progress steal your biological miracle. The time between your first and last breath is your sacred territory. Protect it. Reclaim it. Because, in the end, being the sole owner of your time is the only wealth that survives the collapse of any market. Life is vast, raw, and magnificent, but it only happens to those who have the courage to stop running and, finally, begin to walk on their own.

Printed in Dunstable, United Kingdom